2.

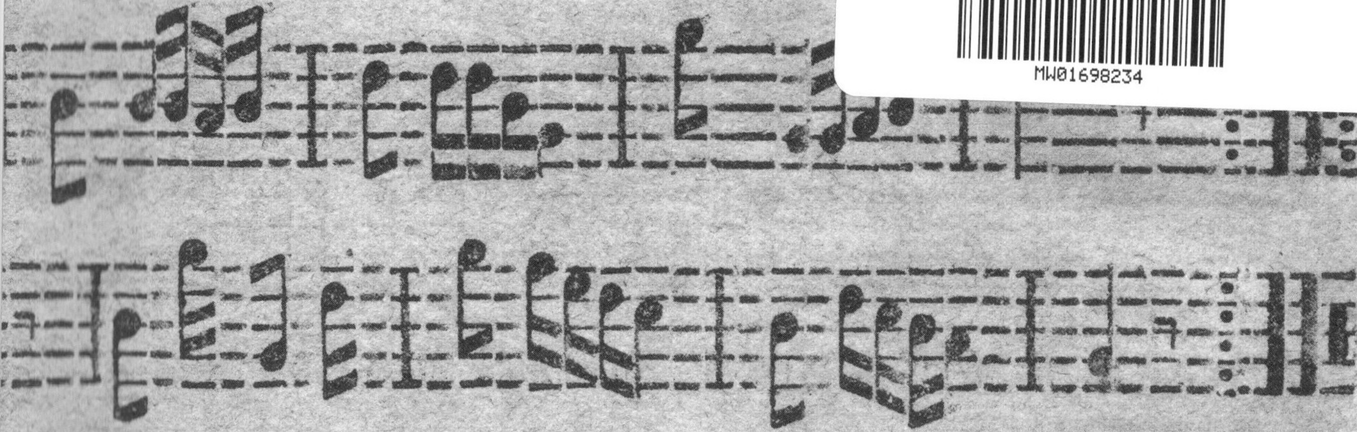

Doodle.

Also known as the Field Music of the Virginia State Garrison Regiment, the Colonial Williamsburg Fifes and Drums have been carrying forward the tradition of military music since 1958.

The Senior Corps is comprised of boys and girls who have passed up to the ranks of corporal, sergeant, and drum sergeant. They march regularly on Duke of Gloucester Street and on Market Square for military reviews.

The drum major provides commands verbally, through hand gestures, and using the mace to indicate what to play, when to play, and what time to keep.

The Junior Corps is comprised of boys and girls who have passed up to the ranks of private, drummer, and corporal. The Junior Corps performs every Saturday.

Regular drills to ensure proper dress and spacing while standing still and while marching require regular individual and section rehearsals. Each corps has two rehearsals a week to practice their music and marching.

The fife is a wooden tube with six finger holes and one mouth hole that the fifer blows across. The fifer can play in a high register to be heard on the battlefield and over long distances on a march or a lower register for entertaining the troops in camp.

Drums belong to the oldest family of instruments. The corps' snare drums are made of wood shells and hoops with calfskin heads and gut snares. Bass drums became popular in Europe around the time of the American Revolution. Americans adopted them as the war continued.

Extra sticks are ornamental and occasionally useful, if a drummer drops one while marching.

Brass ferrules on the ends of the fifes add decoration and keep the wood from splitting.

In the eighteenth century, fifers and drummers served with the enlisted men. One fifer and one drummer were assigned to each company. Fifers and drummers wore the reverse colors of the armed soldiers.

The tempo of the music regulated the pace of the march. A familiar tune on a march could have been "Successful Campaign," "The White Cockade," or "Yankee Doodle."

In camp the soldiers would have heard "The Roast Beef of Old England" to announce mealtime.

Drumbeats could regulate the loading and firing of artillery, including muskets and cannon.

Today's Fifes and Drums appear in over seven hundred performances a year, sometimes as a small group, sometimes as the full corps.

Colonial Williamsburg's musicians honor the men and women of our armed forces by playing at military ceremonies.

During the annual Drummers Call, fife and drum corps from around the world muster in Williamsburg.

DONT TREAD
LIBERTY
VIRGINIA
FOR
CONSTITUTIONAL
LIBERTY

The Senior Corps has performed at venues ranging from naturalization ceremonies to the Macy's Thanksgiving Day Parade.

1440

Fifes and Drums performances are typically a favorite part of special events, like Fourth of July celebrations.

During the annual Grand Illumination, the Fifes and Drums march through Williamsburg surrounded by fiery torches to celebrate the holiday season.

Photographs by David M. Doody and Tom Green

With additional photographs by Barbara Lombardi

Image of sheet music on endpapers from Alvan Robinson,
Massachusetts Collection of Martial Musick. . . . , 2nd ed. (Exeter, NH, 1820), 58.

25 24 23 22 21 20 19 18 17 16   1 2 3 4 5 6

Printed in the United States of America

ISBN 978-0-87935-286-8

Designed by Shanin Glenn

The Colonial Williamsburg Foundation operates the world's largest living history museum—
the restored eighteenth-century capital of Virginia.

The Colonial Williamsburg Foundation
Williamsburg, Virginia
colonialwilliamsburg.org

No.

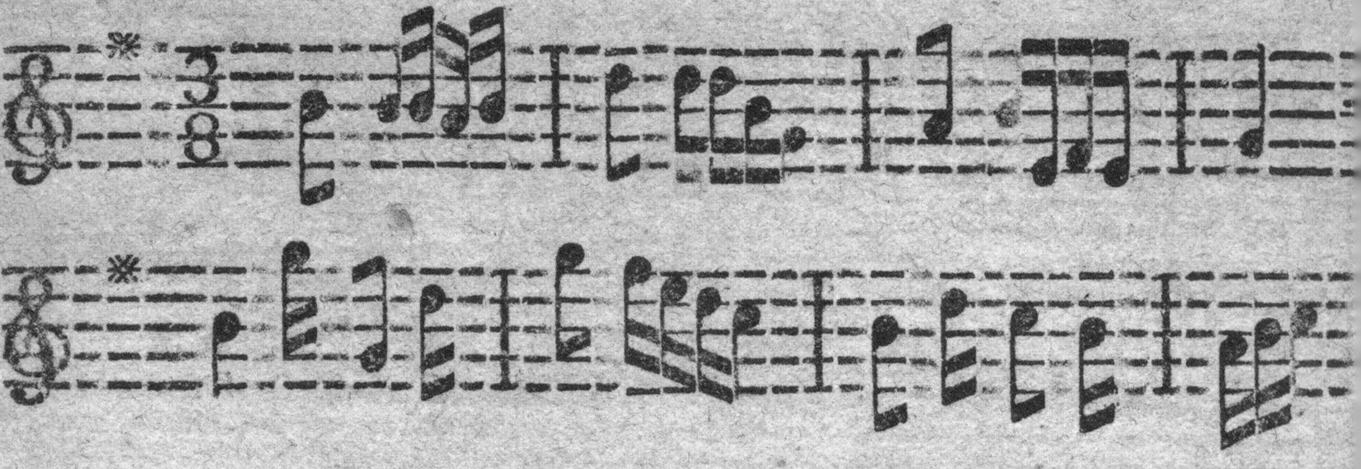

Yankee

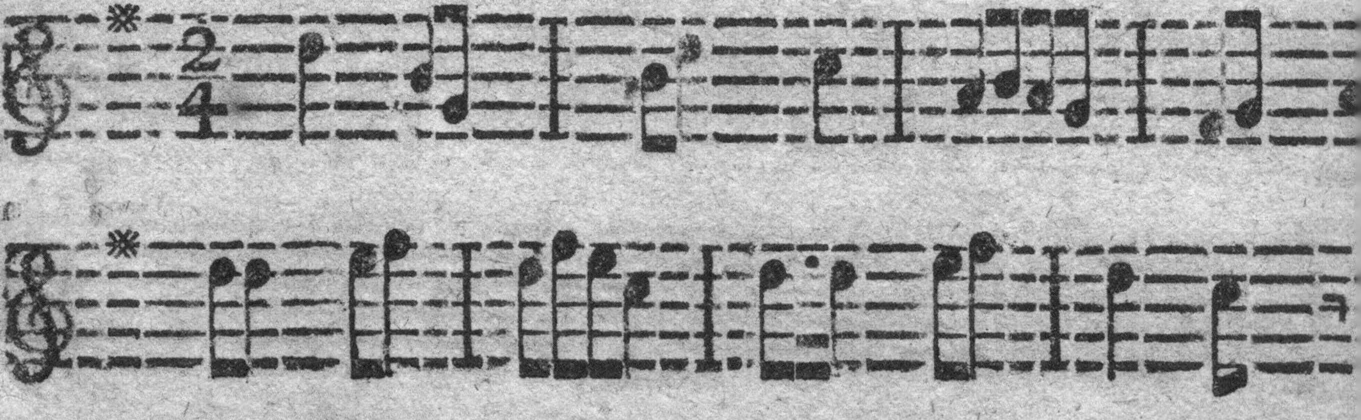